AMAZING MASKS
TO MAKE YOURSELF

25 projects for funny and frightening faces to wear!

Thomasina Smith

ARMADILLO

This edition is published by Armadillo, an imprint of Anness Publishing Ltd, Blaby Road, Wigston, Leicestershire LE18 4SE; info@anness.com; www.annesspublishing.com

If you like the images in this book and would like to investigate using them for publishing, promotions or advertising, please visit our website www.practicalpictures.com for more information.

Publisher: Joanna Lorenz
Editors: Sophie Warne and Richard McGinlay
Photographer: John Freeman
Designer: Edward Kinsey
Production Controller: Mai-Ling Collyer

PUBLISHER'S NOTE
Although the advice and information in this book are believed to be accurate and true at the time of going to press, neither the authors nor the publisher can accept any legal responsibility or liability for any errors or omissions that may have been made nor for any inaccuracies nor for any loss, harm or injury that comes about from following instructions or advice in this book.

Manufacturer: Anness Publishing Ltd, Blaby Road, Wigston, Leicestershire LE18 4SE, England
For Product Tracking go to: www.annesspublishing.com/tracking
Batch: 0343-22667-1127

Introduction

Masks have a long and fascinating history. Their use and meaning varied from culture to culture, but masks have always transformed the wearer. Some were used for rituals and ceremonies in which the wearers were changed into gods and spirits. Others were used on the stage, as in Japan and Ancient Greece. Masquerade was the tradition of using masks in balls and festivals. At the Carnival in Venice, thousands of people still come every year to dress up in fantastic masks and parade the streets.

 The masks in this book are both easy and fun to make. They use all sorts of methods and materials, from papier-mâché to everyday household objects, such as a plastic flowerpot. Masks can be made for all kinds of uses: going to a costume party, for a school production, or even just to hang as decorations on the wall. So, choose a mask and have fun making and wearing it!

Thomasina Smith

Contents

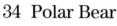

Materials

Although traditional masks use materials like wood and clay, you can make masks from lots of other materials too. Cardboard and papier-mâché are good basic materials, but as you will see, you can also use items such as a plastic ice cube tray or autumn leaves. In fact, almost anything can be useful in mask-making. Start collecting odds and ends, so that you are never short of materials.

SIEVE AND TEA STRAINER

Kitchen supply stores have a good range of sieves and strainers, which are great for mask-making because you can see through them. Plastic ones are better than metal ones, because they come in bright shades and the mesh is made of white gauze rather than metal.

CALICO

Calico is used for the white Ghoul mask, but if you prefer, you can use an old white sheet.

SWIMMING GOGGLES

If you don't already have any swimming goggles, they are easy to find at sports shops. Goggles are fun to use in a mask, and make a cheap substitute for safety goggles too.

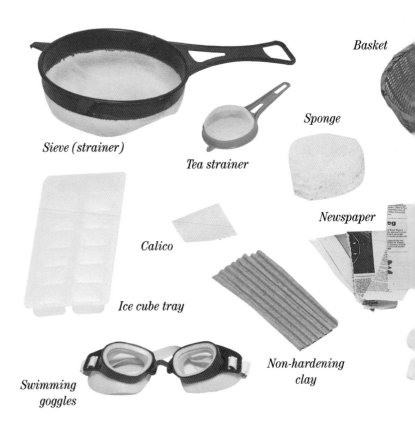

Basket

Sieve (strainer)

Tea strainer

Sponge

Calico

Newspaper

Ice cube tray

Non-hardening clay

Swimming goggles

SPONGE

Use a felt-tip pen to mark out the shape you want on an ordinary bath sponge. Trim using a pair of scissors.

ABSORBENT COTTON

This comes in a number of different forms. Use a roll of it for masks such as Father Christmas.

FUNNEL

Plastic funnels are available in hardware and kitchen stores. They make perfect noses on your masks.

SHOELACES

Why not paint some old shoelaces to make a bright alternative to elastic when attaching a mask?

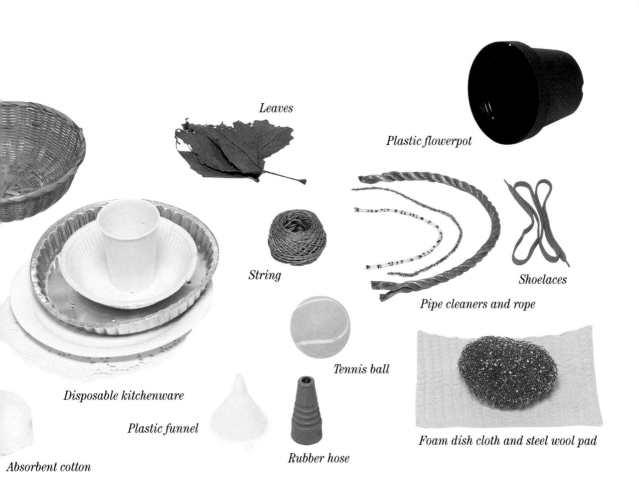

Leaves

Plastic flowerpot

String

Shoelaces

Pipe cleaners and rope

Tennis ball

Disposable kitchenware

Plastic funnel

Foam dish cloth and steel wool pad

Rubber hose

Absorbent cotton

RUBBER HOSE

These are used on the end of kitchen taps and can be found in hardware or kitchen stores. Use them to make great noses and eyes for your masks! Remember, when you are painting on plastic you will need to add white glue to the paint before you start, otherwise the paint will not stick.

TENNIS BALL

If you are making a large mask, such as the Spanish Giant, an old tennis ball cut in half and painted makes a great pair of eyes. Ask an adult to help you cut the tennis ball, as it can be quite tricky to do. Remind the adult to point scissors away from the body.

LEAVES

Use completely dry leaves with edges that have curled up. Handle leaves carefully, as they are very fragile.

PIPE CLEANERS

You can find pipe cleaners in art and craft stores. You can buy plain, striped and glittery ones.

Equipment

All the equipment used in this book is easy to find in art, stationery or hardware stores. Look after your tools and always wash your brushes in lukewarm water with a little soap. Keep your equipment in a box.

ACRYLIC PAINT

Acrylic paints are water-based paints, which means you can wash your brushes in water and you can dilute the paint in water. A cheaper form of acrylic paint is called poster paint.

SPRAY PAINT

You can buy this from art stores. It produces very lively shades, and car spray paint makes a good, cheap alternative. Wear a spray mask and use in a well-ventilated area.

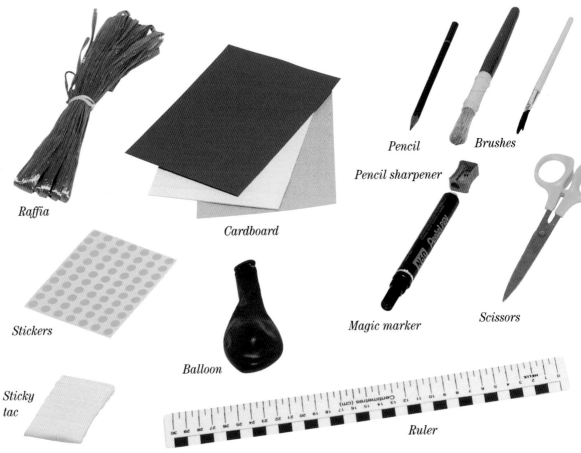

Raffia

Cardboard

Pencil

Brushes

Pencil sharpener

Stickers

Balloon

Magic marker

Scissors

Sticky tac

Ruler

ADHESIVE TAPES

You can use a variety of adhesive tapes. Some types can be found in art and gift stores, but electrical stores also sell a good selection in various shades. Insulating tape is great for holding things together, as it is really strong. Masking tape is useful for temporarily holding things in place when gluing.

SPRAY MASK

You should always wear a spray mask when using spray paint. Spray masks are available in all decorating and hardware stores. The mask has a metal frame with a filter, which stops the tiny drops of paint getting into your lungs when you breathe in. The filter should be changed regularly to remain hygienic.

GLUE STICK

This is great for sticking a flat piece of paper to a flat surface. Smooth out lumps before leaving it to dry. Always replace the lid, as glue sticks dry out.

WHITE GLUE

Also known as PVA glue or wood glue, this takes longer to dry than some glues, but it is very strong.

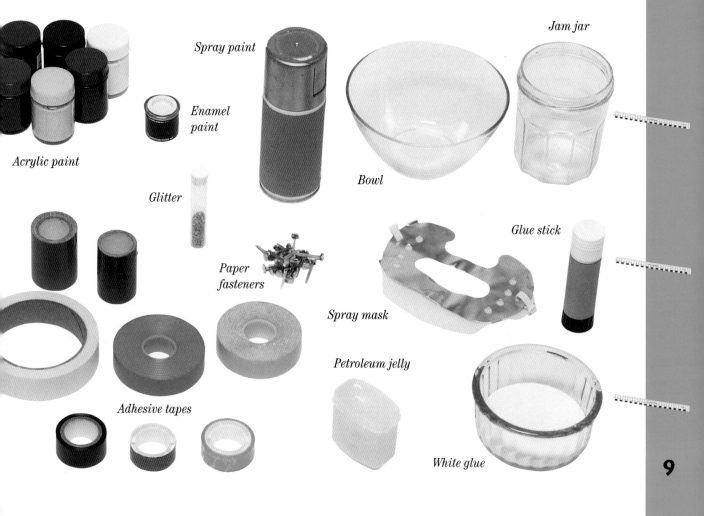

Acrylic paint

Enamel paint

Spray paint

Jam jar

Bowl

Glitter

Paper fasteners

Glue stick

Spray mask

Petroleum jelly

Adhesive tapes

White glue

Papier-Mâché

Several of the mask projects in this book use the technique of papier-mâché. Traditional masks often use wood or clay as their base material. Papier-mâché is a good substitute because you can mould with it and, when it is dry, it is solid and strong. To make papier-mâché, you soak paper in a glue solution. There are several ways of making shapes with papier-mâché. One is to build up layers of papier-mâché on a balloon to make a mask like the Spanish Giant mask. You could also cut the balloon shell in half and use each half to make a different mask.

1 Mix water and glue together. Use one part white glue to one part water. If you plan to make a lot, use a bucket. White glue is much stronger than wallpaper paste.

2 Tear or cut strips of newspaper and soak them in the solution.

3 Coat the balloon in petroleum jelly. You can use lots of different types of moulds to shape papier-mâché – bowls, plates, pans – but always coat them with petroleum jelly first so the papier-mâché is easy to remove when dry.

4 Apply layers of the newspaper to the balloon. After each layer, paste the whole balloon with white glue for extra strength. Leave to dry before you put on the next layer. You will need approximately 3–4 layers.

5 When the papier-mâché is dry and solid, remove the mould. If the mould is a balloon, snip it with scissors and then remove it.

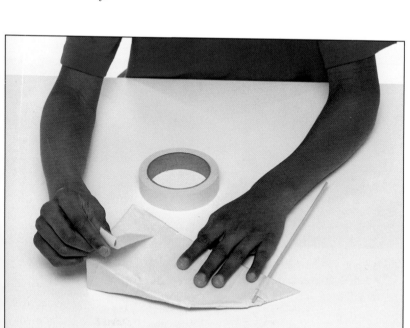

6 Another kind of base for papier-mâché is a cardboard structure. Tape the cardboard to a curved surface with masking tape and apply layers of newspaper as before. This time you don't need to use petroleum jelly. When the final layer of papier-mâché is dry, remove the mask from the curved surface.

11

Basic Techniques

FITTING A MASK

It's a good idea to take measurements of your face when making a mask: for example, the distance between your eyes and from your nose to your mouth, as well as the width around your head. You can draw around a pair of glasses or sunglasses to mark the position of your eyes and the bridge of your nose. This is especially useful for projects like the Venetian Mask.

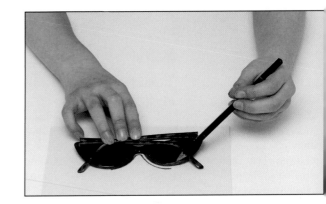

CUTTING EYE HOLES

1 Hold a paper plate or a piece of cardboard in front of your face. Carefully feel where your eyes are using your fingers.

2 When you have found where your eyes are, mark the position of each one with a pencil.

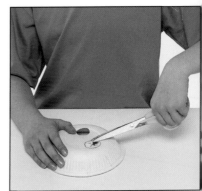

3 Draw two circles. Pierce a hole in the middle of each circle with scissors, making sure the scissors are closed and that your hands aren't in the way. Then cut around the circles.

CUTTING A MOUTH

1 Draw a mouth on the paper plate. To cut it, bend the plate in two and cut across the fold. This will make sure the mouth is even on both sides of your mask.

SAFETY TIPS

1 When cutting any material that might fly up into your eyes, wear eye protection. You can get safety goggles from a hardware store, but swimming goggles make a good substitute.

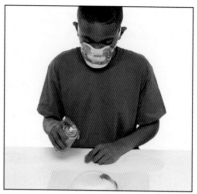

2 When using spray paint, you should always wear a spray mask and work in a well-ventilated room. Don't forget to protect your work surface with scrap paper!

ATTACHING TIES AND STRAPS

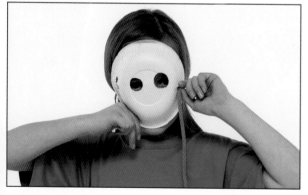

1 There are several ways to hold a mask on your head. The easiest way is to cut two small slits each side of the mask. Tie a strap on one side and fit the mask on your head. Pinch the strap at the length you need.

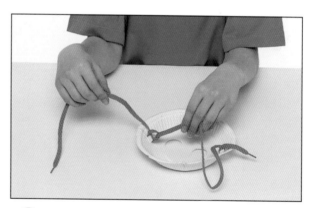

2 Take the mask off, still holding the strap, and mark the place with a pen. Then thread the strap through the slit on the other side and tie firmly at the mark.

Basket Tiger

This idea is taken from traditional African masks, many of which looked like wild animals. The masks were made from natural materials, such as clay and woven grasses.

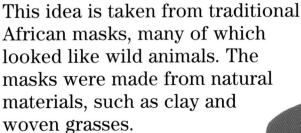

YOU WILL NEED

Basket
Scissors
Pair of goggles or glasses
Thin orange cardboard
Pencil
Scrap of thick cardboard
White glue and glue brush
Acrylic paint and paintbrush
Pipe cleaners
String

14

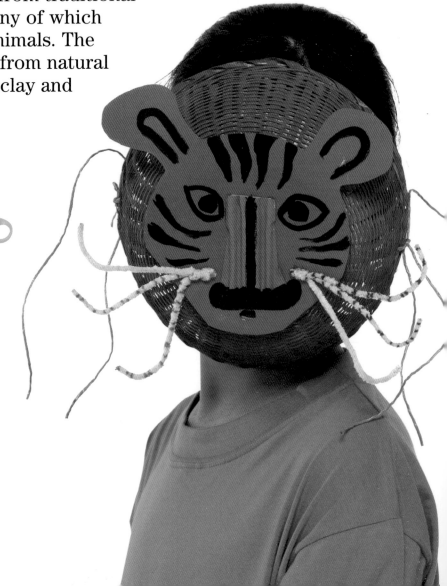

1 Cut a round hole in the bottom of the basket.

2 Place the basket on the cardboard and draw around the hole to make a circle for the tiger's face. Then draw two ears.

3 Cut out the face. Draw and cut out a nose from a scrap of thick cardboard. Glue on the nose and leave to dry. Cut out eye holes.

4 Glue the face to the basket. Leave to dry. Paint the nose orange and decorate the tiger's face with black paint. Glue on some pipe cleaners for whiskers. Leave to dry.

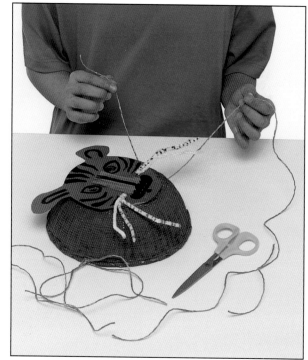

5 Thread string through holes in the basketwork, on each side of the mask. Tie the mask securely around your head.

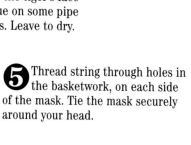

15

Venetian Mask

Venice is famous for its Carnival, when everyone dresses up in costumes and wears masks. Because the mask is on a stick, you don't have to wear it all the time. You can hold it in your hand like a fan.

YOU WILL NEED

Pencil
Cardboard
Pair of glasses or sunglasses
Scissors
Glue stick
Crêpe paper
Doily
Wooden barbecue skewer
   or garden stick
Pipe cleaners
White glue and glue brush

1 Draw the outline of the mask on cardboard, using a pair of glasses as a guide for the shape around your nose. Cut out the cardboard with scissors.

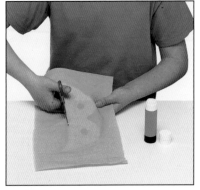

2 Cover the surface of the cardboard with glue and place the crêpe paper on top. Then trim around the edges with scissors.

3 Fold the doily in half and cut out the circle in the middle. Cut the doily in half and fold one half into pleats, like a fan.

4 Using a glue stick, fix the other half of the doily to the mask. Trim it around the edges so that it fits your cardboard.

5 Ask an adult to help trim any sharp ends from the wooden barbecue skewer or garden stick, and wind a pipe cleaner around it. Stick the skewer to the back of the mask with glue and leave to dry for at least an hour. Glue the fan-shaped doily to the top of the mask. Cut a rectangle of crêpe paper and tie it in the middle with a pipe cleaner to make a bow. Glue it onto the mask and leave to dry.

Golden Leaf Mask

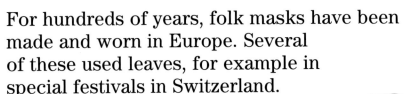

For hundreds of years, folk masks have been made and worn in Europe. Several of these used leaves, for example in special festivals in Switzerland. Masks like the one shown here are still used today.

YOU WILL NEED

Circular foil baking tray
Scissors
White glue and glue brush
Dry leaves
Gold spray paint
Spray mask
Old paper
Wooden barbecue skewer or
  garden stick
Small leaves
Pipe cleaner
Thick electrical tape

1 Carefully cut off the side of a circular foil baking tray.

2 Cover the surface of the baking tray with glue, and cover with leaves. Build up layers of leaves and leave the glue to dry.

3 Spray the mask with gold spray paint. Make sure you wear a spray mask, and spray in a space with plenty of air. If you are inside, open a window. Don't forget to lay down plenty of old paper on your work surface.

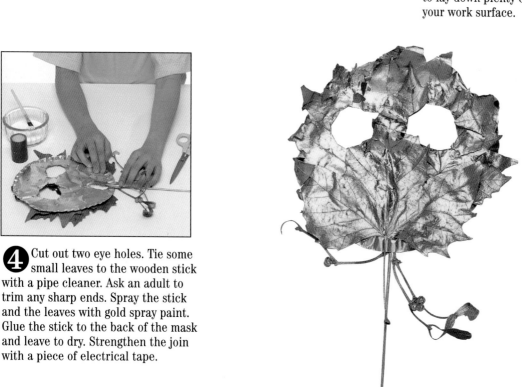

4 Cut out two eye holes. Tie some small leaves to the wooden stick with a pipe cleaner. Ask an adult to trim any sharp ends. Spray the stick and the leaves with gold spray paint. Glue the stick to the back of the mask and leave to dry. Strengthen the join with a piece of electrical tape.

Crazy Glasses

These silly spectacles are inspired by the ones you can find in joke shops. They will give you a truly wacky look!

YOU WILL NEED

Black cardboard
Pair of glasses or sunglasses
Pencil, in a light shade
Scissors
Egg carton
Acrylic paints and
    paintbrushes
White glue and glue brush
Masking tape
Pipe cleaners

1 Draw the glasses shape on the black cardboard, using a pair of glasses as a guide for size and the shape around your nose. You will need to use a light pencil or the outline will not show up. Cut around the outline.

2 Cut out two compartments from an egg carton to make the eyes. Make a hole in the middle of each one for you to see through. Then cut some cardboard from the lid of the egg carton to make a nose. Paint them and leave to dry.

3 When dry, glue the eyes and nose onto the black cardboard glasses. While the glue is drying, it's a good idea to prop the nose up against something and to use a little masking tape to hold it in position.

4 Paint two pipe cleaners black and leave to dry. Apply glue to the ends of the black cardboard glasses. Wrap a black pipe cleaner several times around each end and leave to dry. Bend the pipe cleaners round your ears to keep your crazy glasses in place.

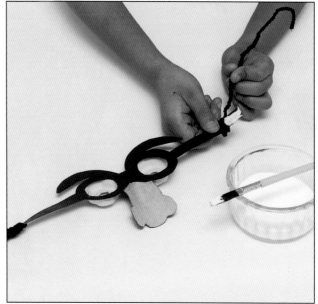

Wicked Witch

Make yourself a scary witch disguise to wear on Halloween. Add a broomstick and you're on your way!

YOU WILL NEED

Paper plate
Pencil
Scissors
Plastic funnel
White glue and glue brush
Acrylic paint and paintbrush
Red paper
Black felt-tip pen
Raffia
String
Thick electrical tape
Elastic

1 Draw a face on a paper plate and cut it out. Cut out holes for eyes. Place the funnel in the middle and draw around it. Cut out the circle, slightly inside the drawn line. Stick the funnel over the hole with white glue.

2 Paint the face green. Mix in some glue to help the paint stick to the funnel. Stick on a small circle of red paper to make a big pimple. Draw in the other features using a black felt-tip pen.

3 Take a big bunch of raffia and tie it together at one end with string. Stick to the back of the plate with a piece of thick electrical tape.

4 Make a hole on each side of the mask. Thread and tie the elastic on one side. Fit the mask on your face and tie the elastic on the other side.

Shining Skeleton

This spooky skeleton glows in the dark and is the perfect disguise to make at Halloween. It glows because it is painted with luminous paint.

YOU WILL NEED

Pencil, in a light shade
Black cardboard
White cardboard
Scissors
Old paper
Small can of luminous paint
Paintbrush
White glue and glue brush

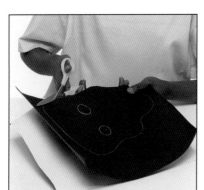

1 Draw a skeleton face on the black cardboard using a light pencil. Hold the black cardboard and the white cardboard together. Cut out the face, including the eyes, cutting through both layers.

2 Trim the white skeleton all around the edge to make it slightly smaller than the black skeleton. Enlarge the eye sockets by about 1cm/½in. Cut out a nose and a mouth. Then cut the mouth off to make the jaw bone.

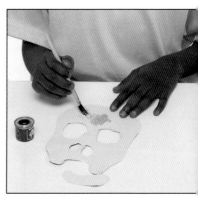

3 Cover your work surface with old paper and paint the white cardboard with luminous paint. Make sure you read the instructions on the can carefully, and use it in an area with plenty of air. If you are inside, open a window. Leave to dry.

4 Glue the white skeleton face onto the black cardboard. Leave to dry. Make a hole on each side to thread through the elastic strap and tie the ends. Now close the curtains, switch off the lights and let the spookiness begin!

Ghoul

Here's another fun mask for Halloween. This ghost is a bit miserable, but you can give yours any expression you like when you cut out the mouth. Happy Halloween!

YOU WILL NEED
Calico or old white sheet
Electrical tape
Black felt-tip pen
Scissors
Scrap of cardboard
White glue and glue brush
Safety pins

1 Put the calico or old white sheet over your head and gently mark the position of the eye holes by placing pieces of electrical tape over each eye.

2 Take the sheet off. Draw an eye hole around each piece of sticky tape with a black felt-tip pen. Cut out the eye holes.

3 Cut out a mouth from cardboard. Add detail with black felt-tip pen and then glue it onto the sheet.

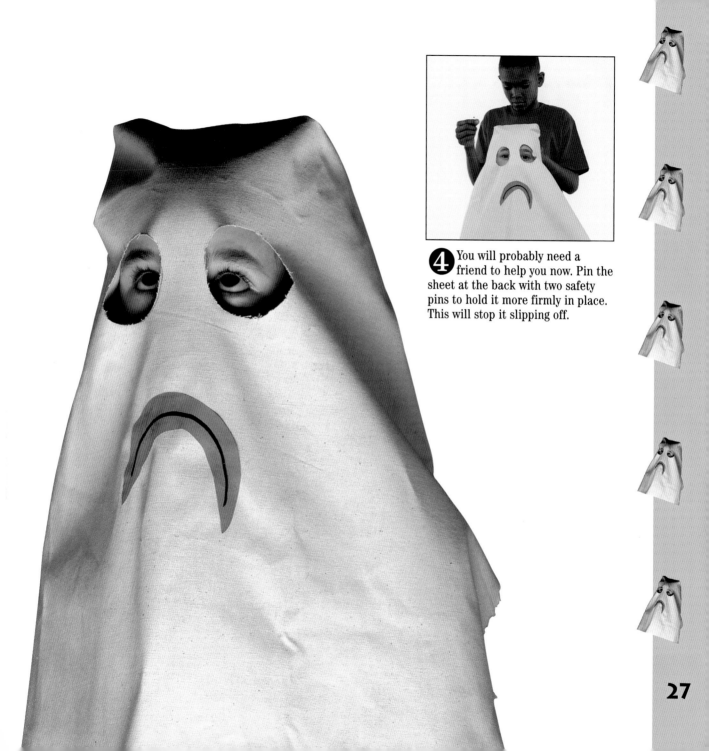

4 You will probably need a friend to help you now. Pin the sheet at the back with two safety pins to hold it more firmly in place. This will stop it slipping off.

Father Christmas

This mask is especially appropriate for the festive season. It will transform you into old man Father Christmas.

YOU WILL NEED

Pencil
Red cardboard
Paper plate
Ruler
Scissors
White glue and glue brush
Red felt
Roll of absorbent cotton
String

1 Draw around a paper plate for the curved part of the beard. Draw a mouth in the beard. Now draw the hat shape. Use a ruler to draw a band 70cm/28in long and 4cm/1½in wide at the bottom of the hat. Cut out the shapes.

2 Spread glue over the hat and lay the felt on top. Don't stick the felt onto the band of the hat.

3 When the glue is dry, cut off the spare felt around the edge of the hat shape.

4 Spread glue on the beard and the band of the hat and lay the cotton roll onto it. Leave to dry. Trim the cotton around the hat band and at the top of the beard.

5 Attach a piece of string to each side of the beard and tie at the back of your head. To fit the hat, wrap the band around your head and mark the join with your finger. Glue the band at the join.

Easter Bunny

Make this fun rabbit mask and use bath sponges for its plump cheeks.

YOU WILL NEED

*Cardboard, in the shade of
   your choice*
Pencil
Scissors
Two bath sponges
Black felt-tip pen
Scrap of black paper
Scrap of white paper
Glue stick
White glue and glue brush
*Six wooden barbecue skewers
   or garden sticks*
Pipe cleaners

1 Draw and cut out a rabbit face, measuring 30cm/12in by 60cm/24in, from cardboard. Cut out two eye holes.

2 Draw two round cheek shapes on the bath sponges and cut them out.

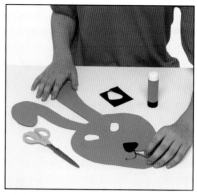

3 Draw a mouth with felt-tip pen. Cut out a nose from black paper and a pair of teeth from white. Stick them onto the mask using the glue stick.

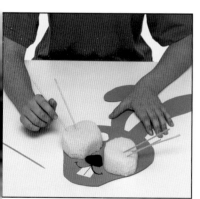

4 Glue on the sponge cheeks using white glue. The sponge will absorb lots of the glue, so be generous with it. Leave plenty of time for the glue to dry. Dab a little glue onto one end of the wooden barbecue skewers or garden sticks. Insert three sticks into each sponge for the whiskers. Ask an adult to trim the whiskers if necessary. Make sure there are no sharp ends.

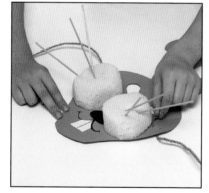

5 Pierce a hole on either side of the mask. Thread a pipe cleaner through each hole and twist the end of it to hold it in place. To wear the mask, hook the pipe cleaners around your ears.

31

Hungry Wolf, Unlucky Lamb

This type of mask is called a transformation mask because it changes from one animal into another. It comes from the north-west coast of America. This mask tells the story of an unlucky lamb eaten by a wolf.

YOU WILL NEED

Two circular foil baking trays
Black felt-tip pen
Plastic cup
Scissors
White glue and glue brush
Acrylic paints and paintbrushes
Black cardboard
Red paper
Glue stick
Thick electrical tape
Pair of shoelaces
Elastic

1 Put one tray on top of the other. Use a black felt-tip pen to draw around a plastic cup in the middle. Cut out a hole for the nose in the middle of the circle. Then make holes for the eyes and mouth.

2 Separate the two trays. Cut one tray in half straight down the middle of the nose and in between the eyes.

  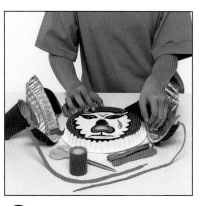

3 Take one half of the tray you have cut in two and stick the plastic cup onto the felt-tip line with white glue. Leave to dry.

4 Paint the tray with the plastic cup nose to look like a wolf. Paint the other tray to look like a lamb. Mix white glue into the paint, so that it will stick to the foil. Cut out two wolf ears from black cardboard and stick on triangles of red paper with the glue stick. Glue the ears to the wolf mask using white glue.

5 Leave the masks to dry, then hinge the wolf mask to the lamb mask with four pieces of thick electrical tape. Close the masks so that the wolf is showing and put tape hinges on the outside as well. With more tape, stick a shoelace to the inside edge of each half of the wolf tray and tie in a bow. Make a small hole on each side of the completed mask for the elastic strap and measure your head before tying both sides.

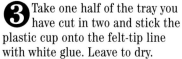

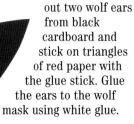

Polar Bear

The secret of making a bear mask is to give it a really good snout. What could be better than a plastic flower pot, with ready-made holes for you to breathe through? If you can't find a flower pot, you can use a yogurt pot and ask an adult to pierce two holes in the bottom.

YOU WILL NEED
Paper plate
Pencil
Scissors
Ruler
White fake fur
White glue and glue brush
Plastic flower pot, 12cm/5in in diameter
Masking tape
Pink fabric
Black and red electrical tape
String

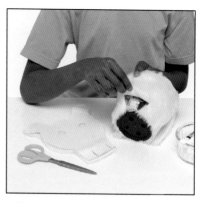

① Draw a bear face with ears on the paper plate. Cut out eye holes. Draw a rectangle 7cm/2¾in long underneath the face. Cut out the face and make four slits in the rectangle. You will use these to attach the snout later.

② Cut a square of fur slightly bigger than the bear's face. Glue it on. Let dry. Cut a rectangle of fur about 2cm/1in wider than the height of the flower pot and slightly longer than the measurement around the top edge of the pot. Cut 8cm/3¼in slits along one long edge of the fur rectangle with an 8cm/3¼in gap between each slit.

③ Trim the fur around the bear's head. Wrap the fur around the pot with the slits at the bottom. Apply glue around the inside edge of the pot, then fold over the fur to stick it down inside. Glue the fur around the outside of the pot – the flaps will overlap where the pot narrows at the base. Trim the fur around the base of the pot.

④ Glue the snout onto the face by sticking the flaps inside the pot. Use masking tape to hold the snout in place while drying. Cut out ear shapes from pink fabric and glue them on. Stick on eyebrows and a mouth in electrical tape.

⑤ Cut the eye holes again. Take a metre/yard of string and thread it through two holes in the bottom of the pot. Then wrap the string around the top of the pot and tie in a knot. Finally, place on your face and tie the strings at the back.

Spanish Giant

This mask is made to sit on top of your head. Material falling from the mask disguises the wearer. Masks like this one are used in Spanish carnivals and are often two or three times the size of a person.

YOU WILL NEED
Balloon
Petroleum jelly
Bowl
Newspaper
White glue and glue brush
Scissors
Tennis ball
Masking tape
Acrylic paints and paintbrushes
Elastic
Nylon net
Fake fur

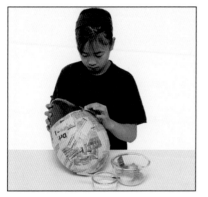

1 Blow up a balloon and cover it with petroleum jelly. Then cover it with several layers of papier-mâché. Leave it to dry until it is solid.

2 Snip the top of the balloon with the scissors and pull it out of the papier-mâché shell.

3 Ask an adult to help you cut a tennis ball in half. Glue the halves onto the shell for the eyes. Use plenty of glue and hold in place with masking tape while drying.

4 Paint the mask. Use a thick brush to put on the base coat and a thinner brush for the details.

5 Once the paint is dry, trim the base of the mask so that it sits firmly on your head. Make a hole in each side and tie elastic onto one side. Get a friend to hold the mask above your head while you fit the elastic strap under your chin. Now tie the elastic on the other side. Tape 2m/2yd of net around the base of the mask for the cloak. Glue on a strip of fake fur to make a collar.

HANDY HINT

When painting the face, make sure you leave enough space under the mouth for trimming the base of the mask. If you prefer, you could fit the mask before you paint it.

Superhero, Master of Disguise

The comic strip superhero flies, defeats evil and is always masked. Is it a bird? Is it a plane? No, it's Superhero!

YOU WILL NEED

Scrap of cardboard
Scissors
Two plastic tea strainers
Clear adhesive tape
Yellow electrical tape
Pair of wool tights
Orange cardboard

① To make the goggles, first cut a piece of cardboard 2cm/1in by 1cm/½in. Stick this between the two tea strainers with clear tape to form a bridge across the nose.

② Bind the bridge with electrical tape. To make a strap to go around the back of your head, cut a strip of tape 60cm/24in long. Place another strip the same length on top, sticky side down. Tape one end of the strap to the goggles.

③ Cut a leg from a pair of large wool tights. Cut a hole half way down the leg, large enough to put your face through. Put it on your head and tie off at the top. Cut the foot off with your scissors.

④ Decorate the top of the helmet with a symbol cut from orange cardboard. Stick it on with electrical tape. Fit the goggles, securing the strap to the other side with electrical tape.

HANDY HINT

Remember that tights are stretchy, so when you make the face hole in your tights, cut a small hole and try it for size. Then make it bigger if you need to.

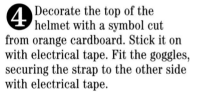

39

Sunshine

This mask is really simple to make! You don't even need any holes for the eyes or mouth – all you have to do is decorate.

YOU WILL NEED

Plastic sieve (strainer)
Acrylic paint and
  paintbrush
White glue and glue brush
Yellow cardboard
Pencil
Scissors
Gold glitter

1 Paint the sieve bright yellow. Mix white glue into the paint to help it stick to the plastic.

2 Draw a circle around the sieve in the middle of a large piece of yellow cardboard. Draw big rays coming out from the circle. Cut out the rays and the circle.

3 Apply some glue to the sieve and the rays, then sprinkle with glitter and leave to dry.

4 Spread glue around the edge of the sieve and push the rays down over the sieve. Leave to dry before holding the mask in front of your face.

41

Coco the Clown

If you enjoy the circus, then you'll love this mask. Use pads of steel wool to make the clown's wild hair.

YOU WILL NEED

Two paper plates
Pencil
Scissors
Acrylic paints and paintbrush
Shiny decorative tape
Raffia
Small plastic lid
White glue and glue brush
Electrical tape
Six pads of steel wool
Paper fasteners
Elastic

1 Cut out two eye holes from one of the paper plates. Paint on your clown face and allow to dry.

2 Draw a triangular hat and a bow tie shape on the other paper plate and cut them out. Paint and decorate the bow tie. Decorate the hat with shiny tape and raffia.

3 Use the plastic lid for the clown's nose. Mix glue into some red paint and paint the nose.

4 Glue the hat and bow tie onto the face and secure on the back with electrical tape. Attach the pads of steel wool to the top of the mask using paper fasteners to secure them in place. Cut a hole in each side of the mask. Tie the elastic on one side, then fit the mask before tying the elastic on the other side.

43

Greek Tragedy Mask

Actors in Ancient Greece used masks with both comic and tragic expressions. Today, these two masks are often drawn together to represent the theatrical arts.

YOU WILL NEED

Paper plate
Pencil
Scissors
Non-hardening clay
White glue and glue brush
Old paper
Gold spray paint
Spray mask
Black paint and paintbrush
Wide ribbon

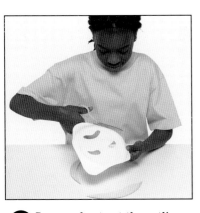

1 Draw and cut out the outline of the face from the paper plate. Cut holes for the eyes and the mouth. Remember to make them look as sad as possible.

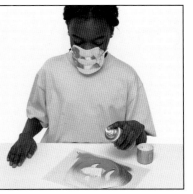

2 Mould a piece of clay into a triangular shape for the nose. Glue it onto the paper plate with plenty of glue. Sculpt the clay so that it is smooth on the plate. Coat with glue and leave to dry.

3 Place the mask on some old paper or newspaper and spray with gold spray paint. Remember to wear a spray mask. Wait a few minutes for the paint to dry.

DON'T FORGET!

When using spray paint, it is best to find a place with plenty of air. If you are inside, open a window. Always wear a mask, which you can buy at any hardware store. Be careful to lay down plenty of paper and avoid places like a brand new carpet or the dining room table!

4 Outline the eyes, mouth and nose using black paint and add lines for the cheeks and eyebrows.

5 Cut two pieces of wide ribbon to make ties for the mask and glue them to the back of the mask using plenty of glue. Leave to dry before tying the ribbons to fit the mask onto your head.

Bush Spirit Mask

Bush spirit masks come from Papua New Guinea. They are made for ceremonies to celebrate the bush spirits, or Kovave. Here is a simple version made from cardboard and fabric. The fringe at the bottom of the mask covers the wearer's shoulders and gives the effect of a bird's body.

YOU WILL NEED

Corrugated cardboard
Ruler
Pencil
Scissors
Masking tape
White glue and glue brush
Rubber hose
Acrylic paints and paintbrushes
Two dried pasta bows
Fabric
Adhesive tape
String

1 Cut the corrugated cardboard into a large square measuring 70cm/28in by 70cm/28in. Fit it around your head and fix the join with masking tape.

2 Glue the cardboard at the join. Leave it to dry and remove the masking tape. Paint the rubber hose brown, adding some white glue to the paint so that it sticks to the plastic. Paint brown stripes on the mask and then paint the spaces white.

3 Using white glue, stick on the rubber hose to make the nose and the pasta pieces to make the eyes. Leave to dry.

4 Cut a piece of fabric 60cm/ 24in by 1m/1yd. Cut it into strips 2cm/1in wide. Attach the strips to a long piece of adhesive tape to make a 1m/1yd fringe. Glue the fringe inside the bottom edge of the mask. Leave to dry.

5 Make two holes on each side of the mask. Thread and tie the string on one side. Put the mask on your head and fit the string under your chin. Tie the string on the other side of the mask.

Crocodile

There is a long tradition in mask-making of using everyday materials from around the home. With this crocodile mask, an ice cube tray takes on a new life!

YOU WILL NEED
Thin cardboard
Ruler
Pencil
Scissors
Plastic ice cube tray
White glue and glue brush
Masking tape
Two dried pasta bows
Acrylic paint and paintbrushes
Green sticky dots
White fabric tape

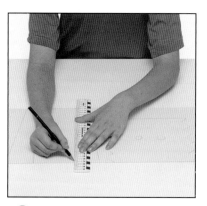

1 For the crocodile's face, draw a square 20cm/8in by 20cm/8in on cardboard. Draw a zigzag line on two edges and two eyeholes. For the snout, draw around the ice cube tray twice on cardboard. Draw flaps around each rectangle to cover the sides and ends of the tray. One rectangle will need a flap on each long side that is wider at one end. Cut around the outlines, leaving tabs for gluing the snout together.

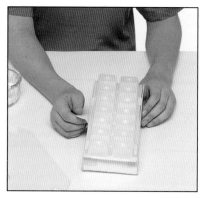

2 Cut out the eyes in the crocodile's face and make two slits for the fabric ties. Use scissors to score along the lines of the snout, remembering to hold the scissors away from you. Fold and glue the tabs. Hold the corners in place with masking tape while the cardboard snout dries. Glue the ice cube tray on top of the snout, using masking tape to keep it in place while it dries. Glue the face to the snout.

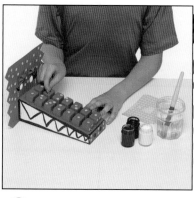

3 Glue two pasta eyebrows onto the face. Paint the crocodile's face and the top of its snout blue. Paint teeth on the sides of the snout. When the paint is dry, add green sticky dots.

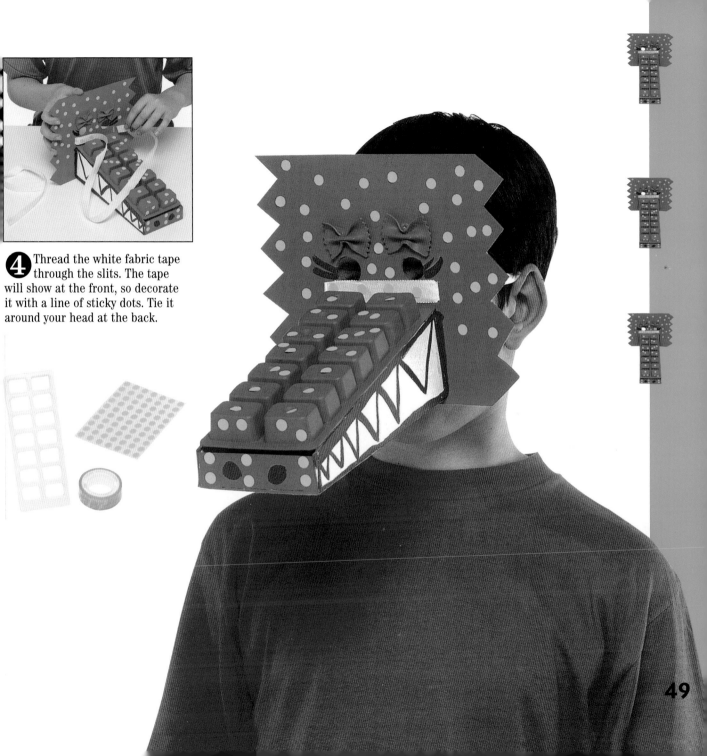

4 Thread the white fabric tape through the slits. The tape will show at the front, so decorate it with a line of sticky dots. Tie it around your head at the back.

Talking House

Not all masks are of animals or humans. It's great to create the illusion of a talking house or a dancing teapot. If you are going to make a matching costume, you could dress all in green, so that your house becomes a house on a hill!

YOU WILL NEED

Cardboard
Ruler
Pencil
Scissors
Acrylic paints and
   paintbrushes
White glue and glue brush
Absorbent cotton
Ribbon

1 Draw a house 25cm/10in by 30cm/12in on a piece of cardboard. Draw in two eye holes and a hole for your nose. Don't forget to add a puff of smoke rising from the chimney!

2 Cut out the house shape. Cut out the holes for the eyes and the nose.

3 Paint the house red. When it is dry, paint the bricks with yellow paint and the other details with black paint.

4 Apply glue to the smoke shape and stick on some absorbent cotton. Paint the smoke a darker shade, if you like. You could also add a cotton tree to the front of the house and paint it green.

5 Make two holes in the mask, one on each side of your head. Thread the ribbon through, starting from the back of the mask and passing across the front. Choose a shade that will blend in.

Beaky Bird

This mask has a beak that moves up and down. The idea came from a ceremonial mask from north-west America.

YOU WILL NEED

Thin white cardboard
Pencil
Ruler
Scissors
White glue and glue brush
Masking tape
Newspaper
Bowl
*Wooden barbecue skewer or
  garden stick*
Acrylic paints and paintbrushes
Orange cardboard
Electrical tape
Elastic

1 Draw the mask pieces on thin cardboard. The mask face should be an oval measuring approximately 30cm/12in by 10cm/4in. You will need two pieces of cardboard for the upper beak approximately 3cm/1in wide by 15cm/6in long. You will also need two lower beak pieces, which should be about 15cm/6in long and 7cm/3in deep. Cut out all the pieces.

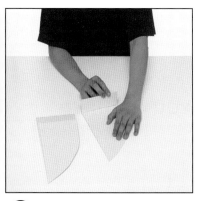

2 Use a pair of scissors to score a flap along the straight edge of each lower and upper beak piece. Remember to hold the scissors away from you. Bend the flaps of the beak. You will need the flaps when gluing the beak.

3 Use the flaps to glue the two lower beak pieces and one of the upper beak pieces together. Bind with masking tape to make a solid box. Cover the beak with papier-mâché. Leave to dry, then repeat. Tape the wooden stick to the beak and add two more layers of papier-mâché.

4 Glue the other upper beak piece onto the face using the flap. When the glue is dry, paint the mask and beak with acrylic paints.

5 Cut out a plume from cardboard and glue it to the back of the mask. Hinge the bottom of the lower beak onto the mask using two pieces of electrical tape, one on the outside of the beak, the other underneath it. Use the stick to move the beak up and down. Attach elastic to each side of the mask to fit your face.

Fish Focals

Masks can be made of almost anything, and from almost anything! Here, a pair of swimming goggles is used to make an underwater mask of a fish swimming through the seaweed.

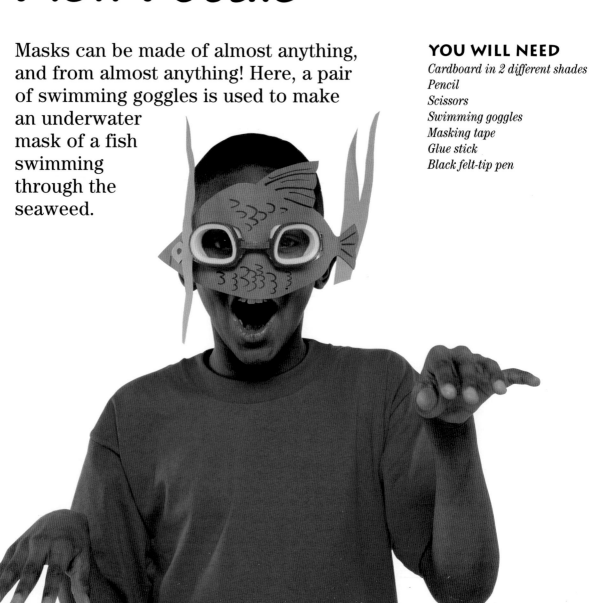

1 Draw and cut out a 25cm/10in by 10cm/4in fish shape. Draw and cut out a small circle for the eye and two pieces of curvy seaweed in a different shade of cardboard.

2 Place the goggles on the fish and draw around the outline. It is easier if you hold the goggles in place with masking tape.

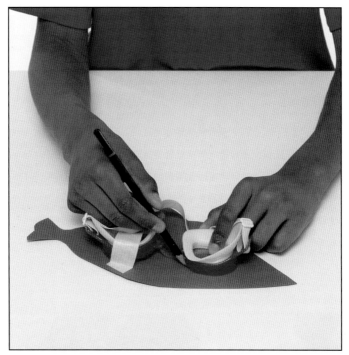

3 Cut out the eye holes. Now cut two small slits, one on each side, to thread the strap of the goggles through. Take the strap off your goggles.

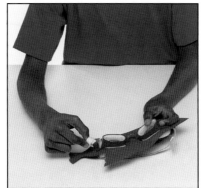

4 Push the goggles into the holes and then thread the strap back through the slits in both the goggles and the mask.

5 Decorate the fish by sticking on the eye and seaweed using a glue stick. Draw on the scales and fins in black felt-tip pen.

55

Happy and Sad Mask

Some masks have more than one expression. This mask has both a happy and a sad mouth. You could also make a mask which wakes and sleeps. To do this, make a set of closed eyes on one stick and a set of open eyes on another.

YOU WILL NEED

Paper plate
Scissors
Acrylic paints and paintbrushes
Pencil
Cardboard
Household cleaning sponge
Two wooden barbecue skewers or garden sticks
White glue and glue brush
Ribbon

1 Cut out eye holes from the paper plate, checking them against your face for positioning. Paint one half of the plate yellow and the other half blue. When the paint has dried, paint on the features in black.

2 Draw a happy mouth and a sad mouth on cardboard and cut them out. Draw around them onto the sponge and cut them out. Ask an adult to help trim the wooden sticks if they have sharp ends. For each mouth, coat the cardboard with glue and sandwich a stick between the cardboard and the sponge. Leave the mouths to dry.

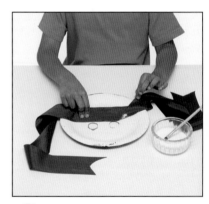

3 Glue a 1m/1yd piece of ribbon onto the back of the mask, below the eye holes, and leave to dry. Tie it in a bow at the back of your head.

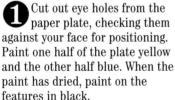

4 Paint the mouths on sticks with red paint and leave to dry. Why not use the mouths to tell a happy and sad story?

DON'T FORGET!

When trimming wooden barbecue skewers or garden sticks always ask an adult for guidance.

Teapot

Here's a fun idea for a tea party – bring your own pot! You'll also get to do some papier-mâché and finger-painting.

YOU WILL NEED

Circular foil baking tray
Scissors
Cardboard
Pencil
White glue and glue brush
Paper fasteners
Bowl
Newspaper
Acrylic paint and paintbrush
Finger paint
Ribbon

58

  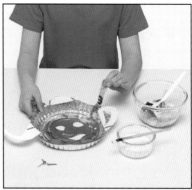

1 Cut out eye and mouth holes in the foil tray. Check them against your face for positioning.

2 Draw the spout, handle and lid on a piece of cardboard. To make sure they are the right size, you can draw an outline around the tray and draw them next to it.

3 Attach the spout, handle and lid to the tray with glue and paper fasteners. When the glue is dry, apply papier-mâché to the joins and leave to dry.

4 Paint the teapot red and leave to dry. Add white spots of finger paint with your fingers.

5 For the mask strap, make two holes approximately 3cm/1in apart on each side of the mask. Thread the ribbon through both holes on one side and tie in a knot at the back. Fit the mask to your head (a mirror helps!) and tie the other side.

COMFORT AND SAFETY TIPS

To make the mask more comfortable to wear, stick tape around the cut edges of the eyes and mouth before you put on the papier-mâché.

Egyptian Mummy

In Ancient Egypt, masks were used for burials. Rich and important people were mummified when they died, and a beautiful mask of their face was made for them to wear. The masks were made from wood and decorated with gold. Here is an Egyptian mask that you can make without having to use real gold!

YOU WILL NEED

Black cardboard
Pencil, in a light shade
Paper bowl
Compass
Ruler
Scissors
Electrical tape and shiny decorative tape
Acrylic paints and paintbrushes
White glue and glue brush
Elastic

1 Draw a mummy shape, about 25cm/10in by 40cm/16in, using a light pencil on black cardboard. Draw around the paper bowl for the face. Using a compass, draw a circle inside the first circle, making it about 1cm/½in smaller. Draw a long, thin rectangle from the smaller circle to the bottom of the mummy shape. Cut out the rectangle and the smaller circle.

2 Decorate your black head shape with stripes of tape. The Ancient Egyptians were fond of gold, red and turquoise shades.

3 Cut out two eye holes from the paper bowl using a pair of scissors. Paint the bowl yellow and leave to dry. Then add the features in black paint.

4 Glue the face onto the decorated head shape. Use plenty of glue and then leave to dry. Pierce two small holes on each side of the mask. Thread elastic through and fit onto your head.

Japanese Noh Mask

One of the most famous forms of traditional Japanese stagecraft is called Noh. This mask is a copy from one of the characters in Noh theatrical art. The Japanese made their masks with wood, but you can use papier-mâché.

YOU WILL NEED

Corrugated cardboard
Ruler
Pencil
Scissors
Saucepan
Petroleum jelly
Masking tape
White glue and glue brush
Bowl
Newspaper
Acrylic paints and paintbrushes
Thick rope

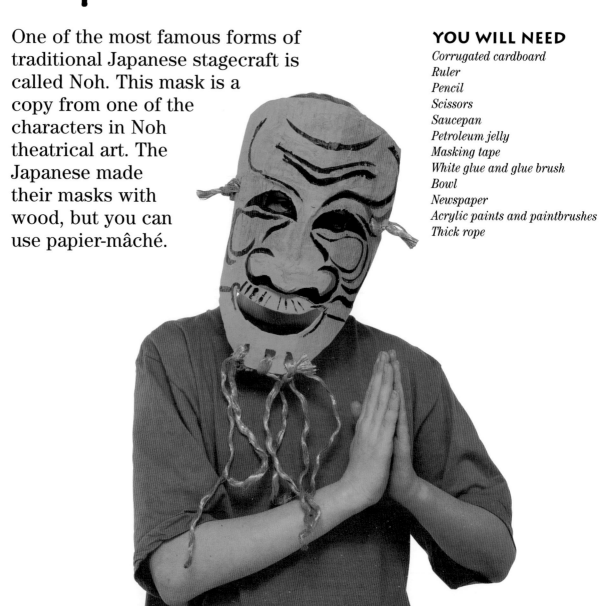

1 Cut out a 30cm/12in by 25cm/10in face shape from corrugated cardboard. Draw eyes and a mouth, checking them against your face for positioning. Cut them out. Now coat the curved outside edge of the saucepan with petroleum jelly.

2 Attach the base of the mask to the saucepan, using masking tape. Apply papier-mâché to the surface of the mask. Leave to dry and repeat. Once dry, remove from the mould and add a third layer. Fold the newspaper strips around the holes to make smooth edges.

3 Mix red and yellow acrylic paint to make an earthy orange. Paint the mask. Leave to dry before painting on black lines for the facial features.

4 Make a beard by piercing three holes in the chin of the mask. Fray the rope and tie two strands through each hole. For the strap, make a hole on each side of the mask. Tie a length of rope through each hole and attach at the back of your head.

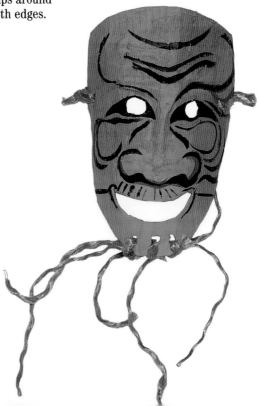

ACKNOWLEDGEMENTS

The publishers would like to thank the following children, their parents and Walnut Tree Walk Primary School, for making this book possible:

Charlie Anderson

Emily Askew

Chris Brown

Chan Chuvinh

Ngan Chuvinh

Isha Janneh

Sarah Kenna

Claire McCarthy

Imran Miah

Marlon Stewart